How to Play the Jazz Trumpet for Beginners

Learn Jazz Trumpet Theory, Harmony, and Techniques from Scratch with Guided Audio Recordings

By: Jason Randall

Table of Contents

Throughout this book, there are musical examples and audio recordings to follow along on your journey to learn how to play the Jazz Trumpet.

Whenever you see the following outline:

> **Audio Examples:** 1-3 Rock Drum Pattern Hi-hat Examples 80-120bpm

Please follow along with the recordings at the Sound Cloud link below or search on Sound Cloud for "How to Play the Jazz Trumpet for Beginners."

https://soundcloud.com/jason_randall/sets/how-to-play-the-jazz-trumpet-for-beginners

Chapter 1

Introduction

So you've gotten the basics of the trumpet down - congrats! You're past the "Hot Cross Buns" phase and playing real songs! Perhaps you've even got a few years playing under your belt, you know, some scales, and hopefully, you've gotten some experience performing live. A great next step logically is to delve into jazz!

Jazz is a classic and rich piece of American history. Like a few other genres, it's a wholly American invention. And the best thing about it? Even if you go years and years without playing jazz, the music theory concepts, muscle memory, and overall skill you develop by playing the genre can transfer over to any other type of music (*regardless* of which instruments you play). It is both advanced *and* palatable enough to really help you improve any style of music you should try out afterward.

But, in order to play jazz, you will first need to conquer the rhythm basis for most of the genre - the "swung" 8th note!

Chapter 2

"Swing" Rhythm

"Swinging" is a term in jazz that refers to a rhythmic way notes are played (or sung); it's so common in jazz that jazz (as a genre) is often just called "swing" (hence the name of offshoot genres, like "electro-swing," which incorporates old-timey jazz samples into EDM production elements). However, this rhythmic pattern is far from exclusive to jazz (or "swing") music - you can find it in plenty of other contemporary genres. But it's near-*ubiquitous* in jazz.

By now, you're familiar with 8th notes and 16th notes. The way you've learned them so far is to play them "straight" - in other words, evenly spaced. As you already know, the pulse of a piece of music is usually represented by "quarter notes" (although not always). 8th notes are twice as fast as quarters, and 16ths are four times as fast (everything is measured against the quarter note, as they represent the "beat" of a song). But what if these notes were *un*even?

In jazz, we typically use **swung 8ths**. Quarter notes still represent the pulse of the music, but the 8th notes are uneven. If we count the usual 4/4 quarter notes "1, 2, 3, 4," and 8th notes "1 and 2 and 3 and 4 and," which is often written as "1 + 2 + 3 + 4 + ." So we'll count everything the same - but the "and" *will all be late*. Instead of them sitting halfway between the "downbeats," they land about two-thirds of the way after the beat and only one-third of the way *before* the beat. Essentially, they're not even 8th notes; they're actually **8th-note triplets**, with the middle triplet removed. These can also be called "broken triplets."

You can hear these differences in these audio examples - this is just a stock MIDI drum kit in Logic Pro over a metronome at 120 bpm, 100 bpm, and 80 bpm. The drums will start with a quarter-note count-in, go to a very simple quarter-note rock beat, then to a straight-8th rock beat, followed by a shuffle that includes every possible 8th-note triplet. Then, the next beat will remove all the middle triplets, leaving the shuffle-y, broken triplets of a swing beat. Just to hear the contrast, it'll wrap up with a straight 16th note beat on the hi-hats.

Audio Examples: 1-3 Rock Drum Pattern Hi-hat Examples 80-120bpm

You may not have any interest in playing the drums, but we might as well also use this time to cover how the swing drum beat is made from these swung eighth notes as well. Regardless of what type of jazz you want to play, you'll be leaning on the rhythm section to feel the groove.

The previous audio examples were based on a traditional rock beat, but jazz drums are traditionally built from the top down. In other words, more emphasis is placed on the ride cymbal than the kick drum. The typical ride cymbal pattern used in jazz starts with a quarter note, then it's followed by a pair of that broken-triplet "swung 8ths" we mentioned earlier. The result, as it's taught in beginner jazz drum lessons, sounds like "Ding, Ding-gah-ding," with that last "ding" replacing the first one. In essence, "ding-gah-ding" is what the pattern ends up feeling like in the drummer's hand once it gets going (because the swung 8ths run straight into the next quarter). Here's how it's built (this audio example starts at quarter notes on the hi-hat, then fills in *all* the triplets on the hi-hats, then overlays the actual swing pattern on a ride cymbal, then turns the hi-hats into the actual traditional jazz hi-hat pattern - played on beats two and four with the drummer's foot). It also includes some typical, simple kick and cross-stick plus hi-tom "comping" from the drummer (again, I've included examples at 80, 100, and 120 bpm, all with a metronome):

One quick clarification, though. This "broken triplet" version of swung 8th notes is just one version. "Swinging" really just refers to a quality that can exist in various intensities - that quality is "offbeats *being late*." So, in this swung 8th-note version, the "and's" is late. But *how* late they are can vary, depending on how "hard" the swinging is.

Sometimes, the intensity of the swing isn't even quite the same between different instrumentalists, thus adding a bit of push and pull. One of my favorite jazz songs, Lee Morgan's "The Sidewinder[1]" always impressed me as having this feel - but as I listen to it now, everyone seems to be swinging the same amount. Regardless, "swinging" is a quality that exists on a spectrum, from "straight" to "heavily swung."

In fact, both analog and VST drum machines used for electronic music production often will have a "swing" knob that can be dialed up or down for intensity. Here's an example of a

---

[1] https://www.youtube.com/watch?v=qJi03NqXfk8&ab_channel=JazzTuna

digital drum sequencer adding swing in that fashion. However, it's doing so with swung 16th notes instead of 8ths.

Swung 16ths are more often found in other genres. This includes some funk and hip-hop. In this situation, the 8th notes are still even/straight, but the 16th notes are now uneven. If the 8th notes are counted as "1 and 2 and 3 and 4 and," - again, notated "1 + 2 + 3 + 4 + " - then we notate 16th notes as "1 ee and ah 2 ee and ah," and so on. Which we can shorten to "1 e + a 2 e + a 3 e + a 4 e + a." For swung 16ths, all of the numbers and "ands" (i.e., the 8th notes) are on time, and all the "ee's" and "ah's" are late - again, with the formula of broken 16th note triplets. So, get 16th note triplets - notes that are three times as fast as eighth notes - and then remove the second triplet. For a semi-contemporary example of a song with swung 16th notes (that **couldn't** be avoided in the zeitgeist several years ago), check out "Stressed Out" by Twenty-One Pilots. But we'll also construct how this works in the following audio example (this is almost always done at slower tempos to accommodate for the swinging of such a fast subdivision, so we'll include all three tempos again (80, 100, and 120 bpm), but know that this style is rarely played in songs faster than 120 bpm (whereas swung 8ths are often played *much* more quickly). Since these are often used in funk songs, we'll build them off a just slightly syncopated drum beat (in the kick drum). These audio examples start with quarter notes on the hi-hat, build to an 8th note funk/rock beat, and then the kicks and snares drop out to expose the newly-added 16th note triplets - the basis of the swung 16th notes. Then, those will turn into swung 16th notes, and then we'll add the kick and snares back in.

> **Audio Example:** 7-9 Swung 16th Drum Beat Construction 80-120bpm

As I mentioned, swung 16th notes are generally only going to go with funk, hip hop, R&B, etc., as they rely on a heavy backbeat on 2 and 4. So, going back to straight-ahead, "swung-8th-note" jazz, here's one more though. As the tempo increases in this style, the ability to perform swung 8th notes on the ride cymbal by a drummer diminishes, so breakneck speeds[2] are played with an even 8th note for *everyone* in the entire band. Which leads us to our next chapter - what kinds of jazz bands can you play in?

---

[2] https://www.youtube.com/watch?v=Pse9wHphsPI&t=23s&ab_channel=davdev89

Chapter 3

Different Types of Jazz Bands and Settings

Jazz is often played in two formats or by two types of bands. The first is the traditional jazz "Big Band" setup. It revisits the glory days of Duke Ellington or Benny Goodman when jazz was the pop music of the time. It was started in the 1910s but reached saturated popularity in the '20s through the '40s. If you join the "Jazz Band" at your local high school, this is the layout you'll probably have.

A Big Band, or "Jazz Orchestra," consists of these sections - Trumpets, Trombones, Saxophones, and a Rhythm Section. In the early days of the Big Band, there would be three or so members per section - but now, the breakdown typically looks like this:

- 5 Trumpets - standing in a row in the back

- 5 Trombones - sitting in front of the trumpets

- 5 Saxophones - sitting in front of the trombones

- The Rhythm Section (consisting of a Drummer on "Trap Set," a Bassist, a Pianist, and optionally a Guitarist) - often set up off to the side of the rest of the band

The **drummer's** "trap set" is really just an antiquated way to refer to the modern drum set. The bassist will likely play an upright, "double"-bass, as seen in classical orchestras. Since the guitarist is optional, this totals 18 people, or "pieces" (sans guitarist).

Big Bands provided the soundtrack to the era's dance music, and the *size* of the band gave large amounts of energy despite the technical limitations of that era's primitive microphones. Nowadays, with tons of new genres to compete with (and far more advanced technology), big-band jazz seems like a bit of a relic simply due to the logistics of transporting (and paying) an 18-piece band. That's why you also don't see many bands like The Polyphonic Spree in rock music, either. Nonetheless, big bands still exist, especially in the armed forces; they're a staple of classic Americana.

Small group jazz, played by "Jazz Combos," consists of simply one to three horn players (trumpet, sax, or trombone) and the rhythm section. They often play a more improvisatory style of music using simple "lead sheets," which contain the main melody and general chord structure of a song (more on that later).

Big band jazz will contain improvised solos, but the song structures are much more planned out and thoroughly arranged. It even will often contain "soli" sections in its music, where one of the instrumental groups (often saxophones) plays a chunk of music with intricate, technical rhythms. Everyone in that group will play the same exact rhythms but with different, harmonized melodies.

Big band jazz orchestras are also the center of attention when they play a concert, while small jazz groups can be "background noise" for cocktail parties - or they can *instead* be the center of attention - much like a DJ, in terms of versatility. Most modern jazz is made by small groups (outside of legacy, institutional acts such as the "Jazz Ambassadors," aka U.S. Army Field Band, or college big bands like the University of North Texas "One O'Clock Band").

What you actually *do* in a small group will be different from your job in a big band jazz setting - so let's visit those differences now.

Chapter 4

Roles within the Traditional Jazz "Big Band"

In any big band situation, the main melody of the song itself will largely be played by saxophones, with punchy background harmonies provided by trumpets and trombones. Sometimes, this approach is reversed, although that's a rare situation. Or, the melody may be interwoven between all the different instruments. But trumpets will usually play melodies less often than saxophones.

As the providers of punchy accents, having a solid range will be key. I'd recommend this <u>range of exercise</u>[3] to keep you in shape. This "punchy accent" role also means less sustained playing for longer periods of time. And often, sustained playing, when it *does* happen, will sit in a lower register as a background instrument. So, your range will naturally improve simply by playing in a big band. Even if you use some negative crutches to get your high notes (like using too much pressure on your embouchure), you can get through the punchy bits - like someone trying to increase their running endurance by using short sprints and then lengthening those sprints over time. And the lower background parts are like *actual* endurance running.

Slight aside: *big band* jazz staccatos (which we will cover later in "Jazz Articulation") will actually make playing high for short, punchy accents *easier.* I regularly see students struggle to play high jazz trumpet parts, only to find how quickly their range and note speed "improve" when they use the right articulations.

---

[3] : <u>https://www.youtube.com/watch?v=21kG_dAen58</u>

As mentioned, there are usually 4 or 5 trumpets in a traditional jazz "Big Band." While the entire trumpet section may or may not play the main melodies and themes of the song, the 1st trumpet is likeliest to do so (obviously). The 1st trumpet, or "lead" trumpet, is *required* to have impeccable range. The 2nd, 3rd, and 4th trumpets harmonize with the 1st trumpet - these harmonies can become pretty deep into the weeds, extending out into chords with 7s, 9s, 11s, and 13s (more on that later). Due to that, while rhythmic precision is a must, *pitch* inaccuracy may easily go unnoticed in certain situations. All jazz is great at reinforcing the idea that mistakes are just blips in time - keep going, and don't look back.

The 2nd and 5th trumpets are slightly unique. The 5th trumpet is an optional role that involves playing the 1st trumpet lead lines down one octave. If they are proficient in their range, they may also step in temporarily as the 1st trumpet if the go-to lead player has run out of endurance (since the 5th trumpet will have the most left-over endurance, as they were playing the lowest parts). Other players can also step in for the lead parts if need be.

The 2nd trumpet is generally tasked with taking any improvised trumpet solos. Or, rather, the best soloist in the section is generally given the seat of 2nd chair (which is a misnomer since the whole section traditionally stands up while playing). So, the 2nd trumpet will need to have a decent range, solid note accuracy, and the ability to perform improvised solos. Clearly, I have a biased affinity for this role, as it's the one I held at all the higher levels of *my* big band experience. It's also the most transferable set of skills for the small-group jazz experience.

Chapter 4.5

Role within the Small Jazz Group

Not every small jazz group needs a trumpet player, but every jazz trumpet player can find themself at home in a small group jazz situation. As mentioned earlier, you can play this style with lead sheets (or from memory). A typical lead sheet only features the main melody of a song, as well as chord changes above the melody.

Small jazz group jazz often follows this formula with the lead sheet:

- Everyone plays the "head" once - as in the main melody of the song.

- Likely, the melody of the song is played a second time, although this *can* be optional.

- Then, as many musicians as the band decides will take an improvised "solo." The rhythm section continues playing the "chord changes" of the song, but no one is playing the melody. Often, every horn player will take a solo, and rhythm sections can optionally take one, too (the piano player is the most likely to get chosen for this, as it's the most purely melodic of the rhythm section instruments).

- Then, to close out the song, everyone plays the "head" together 1-2 times, with the ending either pre-planned or agreed upon at the moment with body language. One of the beautiful things about jazz is the communication it requires.

On that note, this genre of jazz generally requires more improvisation on *everyone's* part - not just the horns. Even when not performing an improvised solo, rhythm section members often bounce ideas off other soloists - they call this "comping" for drummers, for instance. This name comes from the idea of "complementing" the musicians around you - being the puzzle piece that fits musically with what they're playing at the moment. There can be an element of call and response or even trying to predict what others will do and copy them in real time. Maybe the rhythm section players will just tastefully fill in the gaps in someone's solo. It's like a conversation - pretentious as that may sound - but it feels free, open, and loose. You'll even see musicians "quote" certain famous beats or melodies that act as in-jokes to others in the group.

Small group jazz doesn't have to follow this formula in arrangement but often will stick to this *instrumentation* (even if it's augmented with electronics or other slight variations). Whether you're playing in a small group or a big band, you'll want to familiarize yourself with jazz stylistically and know how to play the parts authentically for the genre - this is largely covered through a specific style of *articulation*.

Chapter 5

Jazz Trumpet Articulation

Articulations on the trumpet are slightly different in jazz than in classical or concert band music. Some of it lines up with the articulating style in the pep band, but it still has its own overall style.

Jazz features plenty of legato sections, which require a very light tongue. For this style, it helps to think of your airstream into the trumpet as water coming out of a hose - it's constantly on, and your tonguing just acts like a finger gliding against the hose's stream of water (or air in the trumpet version of this metaphor). "Swinging" is also helped in these legato sections with a slight "mini-accent" on the offbeats (or "ends"). This is especially prevalent for saxophone players but also affects trumpets sometimes.

Speaking of accents, there's a great guideline for extra accents in jazz music. In big band music, accents will likely be notated. But still, this rule of thumb will go far - in every musical phrase, add an accent to the **first** note, the **highest** note, and the **last** note. This goes for every larger musical phrase of 4 to 32 bars but is also true for "mini" phrases inside of the bigger musical phrase. This gives us a sort of "matrix" of accents on top of accents within an entire piece of music and helps give jazz its feel (loads of these accents will also land on the "offbeats," further adding to the song's "swing").

But we didn't cover those "punchy accents" mentioned earlier that trumpets add to big band music. Traditional trumpet technique tells us that even staccato notes rely on the tongue to start the note, and a short puff of air propels the note for a smaller duration. In big-band jazz, this isn't always true. We regularly need to have fat, punchy notes that are *still* staccato. We can achieve this with what's called a "tongue stop."

Simply put, you start the note with a hard tongue, like a typical, traditional *marcato* (which, to oversimplify, is basically an accent on top of a staccato). Then, you use a steady stream of air, *unlike* a classical staccato. But, unlike any of the usual suspects in traditional articulation, you *stop* the note with your tongue **again**. To put this in phonetic terms, the articulation would sound something like "TahT."

These sound great *and* will help save your air supply. As mentioned earlier, students often see an immediate "improvement" in their range and endurance once they utilize this technique. I use quotes around the word "improvement" to signify that, really, better range and endurance are just being *revealed* thanks to the new technique.

Utilizing the extremes of the swung legato and tongue-stopped marcato will really make a huge difference in stylistic authenticity for jazz and funk music - and, to reiterate one last time, make both *easier to play* in the process. You can hear this style of accenting and articulation in this playthrough of "Au Privave":

Audio Example: 10. Au Privave Play Along

So, what are some common arrangement styles in these genres?

Chapter 6

Common "Forms" in Jazz Music

We've covered the overall *song* form used in small-group jazz combos, but what about the song form of big-band jazz? Better yet, what are some common "forms" or common arrangement layouts for the "head" itself? There are a few very common forms for the "head" of a song, as well as a pretty common form of the overall song in *big band* jazz.

Let's start with a common overall song format for big-band jazz. It's not dissimilar to the lead sheet, small group jazz format. Songs may start with an intro, which could be 4 or 8 bars or one full-time through the head. This could be played exclusively by the rhythm section in a chill, "vamping" style of playing. For instance, the drummer may only be playing a swing beat on the hi-hat. Or, the intro may include rhythmic "hits" by the rhythm section, matching rhythms in the melody. A sort of combination of these styles can be heard in the intro to "Take the A-Train," which features a melodic section that's *not* part of the main head.

After the intro, the head might be played once or twice, with some arrangement changes on the second time - there could be more rhythmic accents by background instruments (i.e., whoever isn't playing the head). Then, the song will likely open up for a solo section, where soloists each take their turns playing over the rhythm section. So far, we're nearly identical to the song format of small-group jazz.

Then, optionally, the arrangement may call for a soli section - the coordinated, harmonized "solo" (not improvised) played by an entire section (often the saxes). After that, it's back to playing the head again. Around this time, we might end up with a "shout chorus," which is the main departure from small group jazz (outside of *soli* sections).

A "shout chorus" consists of 1-2 times through the head but with extra, bombastic energy. The rhythm section will play a simpler, more driving groove - the drummer may even play powerful quarter-note kick drums and a heavier beat (not unlike the "four-on-the-floor" kick pattern of modern house music). This is the time for the arranger to pull out all the stops - accents in the trumpet section will be extra punchy, high, and lively. You'll be well-rested from the optional solo and sax soli sections, so this is the time to blow out your lips to make sure you hit those notes! But with a proper embouchure, of course!

Many songs end on the shout chorus, and some will end with some sort of coda/outro or just one more relatively relaxed take on the head.

But what about a few common "forms" in jazz *within* the head? Let's examine a couple of those now.

The **AABA** Form

The AABA form is somewhat self-explanatory. One melodic idea and set of chords is played twice, then a different "bridge" or B-section is played, and then the first idea is played again. This entire package is required to play through the head *once*. "Take the A-Train," mentioned earlier, follows this form. Usually, each A and B section is 8 bars, added to a 32-bar form.

In small group jazz or in solo sections in big band, it can be easy for soloists to get lost - especially if their solos last for more than one time through the form. The three consecutive A sections - the last A from one time through, followed by the first two As on the next time - are an easy trap to lose your bearings. But hopefully, the rhythm section will help you navigate this by accentuating the beginning of the new form (i.e., the second of the three "A" sections).

The 12-Bar Blues

The 12-Bar Blues is a classic form, and it's another purely American invention. For how conventional, common, and timeless it is, it's also a bit strange. Music of all kinds tends to follow a four-bar-phrase format, and the 12-bar Blues is no exception. But that's what makes this style unusual - there are *three* of those four-bar chunks in the entire 12-bar form. So it's asymmetrical, with an odd number of four-bar chunks, thus making it another possible trap for soloists.

The 12-bar Blues can be in minor or major, but here's a major-key version of the chord progression:

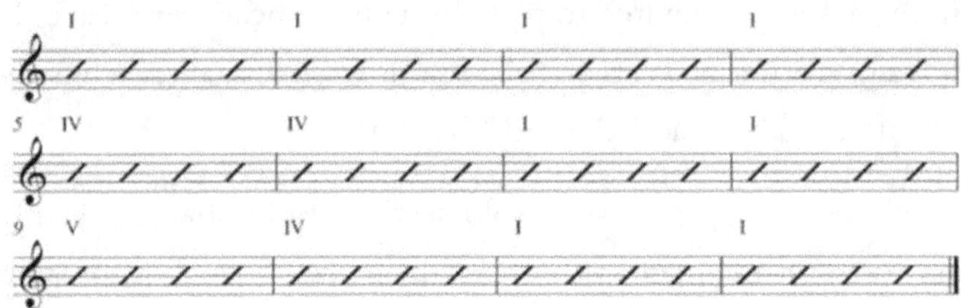

There are some common variations of this form, but this is the most basic version. These numbers represent which chord is being played - each number represents a chord based on that degree in the scale of the song. If you're in C major, then the "I" chord is C, the IV chord is F, and the V chord is G. Often, there will be a 7 after each chord, indicating that each of them is a "dominant" chord (more on that later).

Some variations include putting a V in the last bar, an IV in the second bar, a #IVdim in the 6th bar (e.g. an F#dim if you're in C - for some added blues spice), a III in the 8th bar (e.g. an undiatonic E-major in the 8th bar - which leads nicely to the V-chord in the next major), and, lastly, and optional ii-V-I in the 9th through 11th bars. Don't worry about all that for now, though.

These are all famous jazz songs in the 12-bar blues format (all of which can be found in "The Real Book," which we'll mention later):

C Jam Blues, Straight No Chaser, Blue Monk, Au Privave*

…although there are many more. And all these rock-and-roll songs are also 12-bar blues-es:

Johnny B. Goode, Pride and Joy, Tutti Frutti, Rock and Roll

(*Au Privave is a 12-bar form, but the blues element is nearly erased by the number of ii-V-I turns in it.)

Rock and roll songs are more likely to be in easier keys for guitar, like E and G concert, but since horn instruments are in Bb or Eb, jazz blues songs are more likely to be in keys like Bb and F concert (or C and G to you, fellow trumpeter). So those are great blues scales to familiarize yourself with as soon as possible.

Chapter 7

Improvisation 1: The "Blues Scale"

The blues scale is a magical scale. It just *works*, regardless of which chords are happening in the background (provided you're playing it over a blues song). In fact, it works over both a major *or* a minor blues. It's a slight adaptation of the minor pentatonic scale. For both the minor pentatonic and blues scales, we'll spell it out in the key of our C (or Bb concert) - the first key I'd recommend you learn it in.

The minor pentatonic scale is built off these scale degrees: I - bIII - IV - V - bVII

So, the notes of our C minor pentatonic scale are: C - Eb - F - G - Bb

It's called a "minor pentatonic" because it is only five notes (hence the name *penta*tonic), and it distills our C minor scale into its most concentrated essence. It'll also work over Eb major songs, and guitarists often use this scale (even more so than the blues scale).

The blues scale adds one more note - the "blues note" - which is the #4 (or b5). So, for us, that'd be F#. So, our full blues scale in C is this: C - Eb - F - F# - G - Bb.

Then, simply repeat the scale in either direction (preferably higher when trying to add energy to your solos).

Here's a sample of me soloing over a 12-bar blues using just the blues scale:

<u>Audio Example:</u> <u>11. Bb Blues Solo 1 (Blues Scale)</u>

Let's also transpose this to *our* key of G (or F concert). See if you can transpose it yourself! I'll give you some space so as to not leave any spoilers.

Alright, here's your answer. Our G blues scale is as follows: G - Bb - C - C# - D - F.

These scales and the 12-bar blues both make for a great way to first dip your toes into improvisation. But if you want to go deeper, you'll need to get comfortable navigating chord changes.

Chapter 8

Improvisation 2: Chord Changes

I won't lie to you: playing over chord changes is scary. But it doesn't have to be terrifying, and we can ease our way into it.

By now, you've likely learned your major scales. Hopefully, you've also learned some form of minor scales. There's:

The natural minor, which follows the key signature (minor 6th and 7th notes)

The melodic minor, which has a major 6th and 7th on the way up and flats them on the way down

The harmonic minor, which has a minor 6th and a *major* 7th - leads to a big gap

Minor key songs tend to utilize all of these, but technically, only the natural minor "counts" from a music theory perspective.

Then there's the chromatic scale, which consists of all 12 notes - it's simply half-steps. None of the chords you encounter will be based on this scale, but it's very useful nonetheless.

Next, there's the diminished scale, which consists of alternating whole-steps and half-steps. The chord tones are all minor thirds away from each other. Let's not get too into the weeds of music theory here, but it's a weird scale. The other super weird scale we'll (very rarely) utilize is the whole-tone scale. As it suggests, this scale is purely made of whole steps and forms the basis of augmented chords.

When a chord appears above our sheet music, it tells us what notes are "safe" to play. Of course, we can always decide to ignore these suggestions. But most listeners, no matter how unstudied, can tell whether this is a deliberate choice on our part or if the soloist is struggling to keep up with the changes. Anyway, these chord symbols will basically spell out the scale the soloist should use for that particular chunk of time. We can read these symbols and decipher the scale to use, as well as which notes to accentuate or land on in our improvised musical phrases. Here's a guide that lists all of the common chord changes you'll encounter. For ease of simplicity, let's put every chord type into our key of C.

Let's start with triads - or the most common, basic chords across all genres. They are based on the root, the third, and the fifth of a given scale:

Type of chord	Scale degrees	Chord Notes	Full-scale	Diagram		
Major	1	3	5	(C E G)	C D E F G A B C	C
Minor	1	b3	5	(C Eb G)	C D Eb F G Ab Bb C	Cm
Diminished	1	b3	b5	(C Eb Gb)	C D Eb F Gb Ab Bbb B C	Cdim
Augmented	1	3	#5	(C E G#)	C D E F# G# A# C	Caug

(x = "double sharp," and bb = "double flat" - for all intents and purposes, a Bbb sounds the same as an A, and an Ax sounds the same as a B)

Let's say a C major chord shows up in your lead sheet, and you're improvising over it. You'd want to play a C major scale and "land" on the C, E, and G a bit more often than the other notes.

Jazz chord changes will almost always include extensions beyond these triads. Here's a chart that covers the various 7th chords, etc.:

Chord Type	Formula	Notes	Chord Name/Suffix
Major	1–3–5	C-E-G	C
fifth (power chord)	1–5	C-G	C5
suspended fourth	1–4–5	C-F-G	Csus4
suspended second	1-2–5	C-D-G	Csus2
added ninth	1–3–5-9	C-E-G-D	C(add9)
sixth	1–3–5–6	C-E-G-A	C6
sixth, added ninth	1–3–5-6–9	C-E-G-A-D	C6/9
Major seventh	1–3–5–7	C-E-G-B	Cmaj7
Major ninth	1–3–5–7–9	C-E-G-B-D	Cmaj9
Major seventh, sharp eleventh	1–3–5–7- #11	C-E-G-B-F#	Cmaj7#11
Major thirteenth	1–3–5–7–9–13	C-E-G-B-D-A	Cmaj13
minor	1–b3–5	C-Eb-G	Cm
minor, added ninth	1-b3-5-9	C-EB-G-D	Cm(add9)
minor sixth	1–b3-5-6	C-Eb-G-A	Cm6
minor, flat sixth	1–b3–5–b6	C-Eb-G-Ab	Cmb6
minor sixth, added ninth	1–b3–5–6–9	C-Eb-G-A-D	Cm6/9
minor seventh	1–b3–5–b7	C-Eb-G-Bb	Cm7
minor seventh, flat fifth	1–b3–b5-b7	C-Eb-Gb-Bb	Cm7b5
minor ninth	1–b3–5–b7–9	C-Eb-G-Bb-D	Cm9
minor eleventh	1–b3–5–b7–9-11	C-Eb-G-Bb-D-F	Cm11
minor thirteenth	1–b3–5–b7–9–11–13	C-Eb-G-Bb-D-F-A	Cm13
dominant seventh	1-3-5-b7	C-E-G-Bb	C7
seventh, suspended fourth	1-4-5-b7	C-F-G-Bb	C7sus4
ninth	1-3-5-b7-9	C-E-G-Bb-D	C9
ninth, suspended fourth	1-4-5-b7-9	C-F-G-Bb-D	C9sus4
eleventh	1-5-b7-9-11	C-G-Bb-D-F	C11
thirteenth	1-3-5-b7-9-13	C-E-G-Bb-D-A	C13
thirteenth, suspended fourth	1-4-5-b7-9-13	C-F-G-Bb-D-A	C13sus4
diminished	1-b3-b5	C-Eb-Gb	C°

List of chord types names suffix formulas and notes

You might (understandably) be thinking, "Wait - I need to play a new scale for *every* chord change?????!" I know when I was first tossed into a soloist role in a big band, I felt a great sense of panic and dread. But - most of these chord changes will be largely **diatonic**. In other words, most of the changes will center on the same scale (which is the scale of the song). For instance, let's take a look at "Fly Me to the Moon," a classic Frank Sinatra standard that's listed here in G minor / Bb major:

Fly Me To The Moon

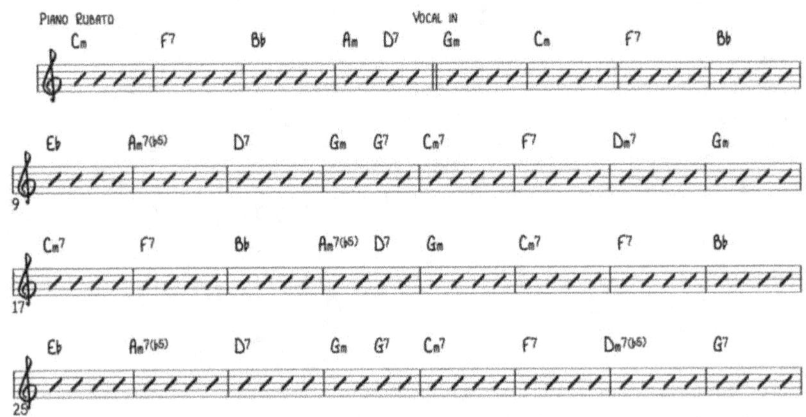

Like "Autumn Leaves," this song features a "Circle of 4ths/5ths" progression. Let's ignore the intro and analyze the first 8 measures after the mark "Vocal in." The vast majority of these chords all conform to the home scale of Bb major / G minor:

Chord/Scale	*Tones*
G minor	G Bb D
C minor	C Eb G
F7	F A C Eb
Bb	Bb D F
Eb	Eb G Bb
Am7b5	A C Eb
D7	D F# A

This chord - D7 - is the first chord to not fit into this scale. The F# sticks out, but only to emphasize the return to G-minor (as the major seventh of the G-minor scale). So, up until this point - you'd want to emphasize these chord *tones* in your playing, but you get to use the same *scale* the entire time.

We don't need to go into too graphic of detail in jazz improvisation here. But the point is, it doesn't have to be as daunting as it looks. Plenty of songs feature far fewer chords and just move short distances modally. Songs like "Maiden Voyage" and anything on Miles Davis' "Kind of Blue" album make for great starter tracks to improvise over (after graduating from both the Blues Scale and actually improvising over the blues chord changes).

On that note (rimshot for the pun), let's talk briefly about improvising over a 12-bar blues using the *actual* chord changes. Here's that form again:

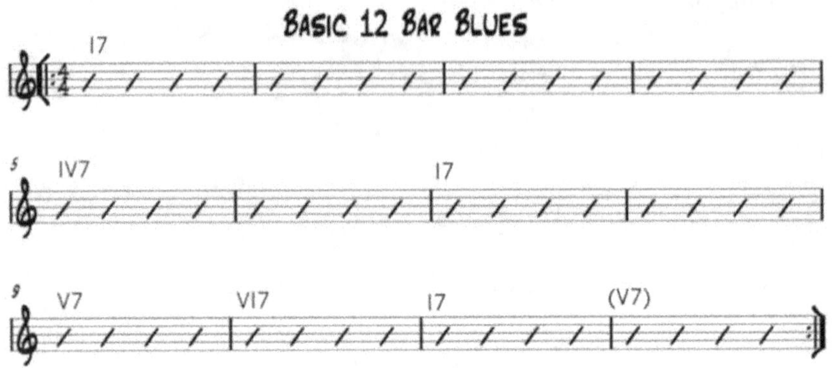

Let's play it in C major. So our chords are thus:

I7 = C7 = **C** D **E** F **G** A **Bb** C

IV7 = F7 = **F** G **A** Bb **C** D **Eb** F

V7 = G7 = **G** A **B** C **D** E **F** G

The chord tones, in bold, are the ones we want to hit more often than the rest. But what's also worth pointing out is which notes *differ* in each chord/scale. Notice that our "one" chord has an E natural, and our "four" chord has an Eb. Spelling out this difference and hitting those notes will make your solo seem more "legit," as you are thoroughly "spelling out the changes." You can take this a step further by making sure to hit the B natural in our "five" chord (as both the I and IV chords have Bb in their scale). Notice also how all of the notes I mentioned are chord tones - so you should be hitting these hard, anyway! This is a much better way to get into improvisation than full charts in other sub-genres, as it's not only (relatively) simple, but also you can always play your

Blues Scale as a backup plan. You can find plenty of free backing tracks to practice this over on YouTube.

Here are a few examples of the Author soloing over a 12-bar blues in our key of C (Bb concert). In each example, I played two choruses for a total of 24 bars. This first example consists entirely of the blues scale:

> **Audio Example:** 11. Bb Blues Solo 1 (Blues Scale)

On that solo, I tried to hit chord tones while still adhering to the blues scale (e.g., on the V chord, I landed on G, as it's the only V-chord note that fits in the blues scale). I went up and down the scale a bit more than I should've, although I broke away a bit from that in the second chorus.

The other examples play over the changes. Notice how, in the second example, I play some Eb's over the C7 (or I7) chord. That rubs against the I7 chord, but it gets grandfathered into the fitting notes thanks to the blues scale. So, an Eb still works on an I7 chord, but an E *doesn't* work over the IV7 chord. All that said, *all of these rules* can be broken with an artistic vision and plenty of confidence. And you can follow all of the rules and still *not* pull off a decent solo *without* confidence. Improvisation requires some swagger - which is independent of shreddy chops. For instance, Miles Davis embodied that swagger without crazy range or technicality.

> **Audio Example:** 12. Bb Blues Solo 2 with Changes

Notice how I also use plenty of repeating motifs and ample rests for taste, rest, and time to think (hopefully, you can get to the point where you *only* use rest for taste). The next version uses motifs, lays way back on the beat, and uses plenty of chromatic scale:

Audio Example: 13. Bb Blues Solo 3 with Changes

On the last solo, I started out strong with a quote, which I used twice for extra emphasis (and time-filling, if we're being honest). The quote is from "Rhapsody in Blue," which I first heard in the movie Fantasia 2000 forever ago. I wanted to include a quote to show how easily they can be implemented - and when I got a little less confident at the end of the solo, I used my good old chromatic scale (with plenty of swagger) to make it to the end!

Audio Example: 14. Bb Blues Solo 4 with Changes

Even in more complex situations, the chromatic scale is a great way to navigate times of confusion. It's an intentionally jarring-sounding scale, so you can use snippets of it to noodle around until you find appropriate chord tones. Don't overuse this crutch (as I certainly have), but it's still a useful tool even if you're not overwhelmed. You can even hear chromatic approaches to chord tones in the melody itself of the original "Overworld Theme" from the "Super Mario Bros." video game series. As one YouTube channel describes it - these chromatic approaches[4] add "playfulness" to the song. If they work in timeless melodies, they'll certainly work in your solos - whether being used to get yourself out of a jam or with actual musical intent!

Little known fact (to the general public, at least): these classic video game soundtracks were not only heavily inspired by jazz, they actually straight up plagiarized 80s jazz fusion records[5] of the time period. Just thought I'd point that out in case Nintendo has any problems with their music being mentioned here.

One more thing to keep in mind when soloing - it's generally considered a great strategy to build your solo over time, with the increasing intensity coming from more (or faster) notes, higher notes, more technical playing, and so on. So remember to leave plenty of space when necessary earlier in your solos for this contrast. This will also appease the "jazz is all about the notes you *don't* play" crowd and comes across as "tasteful." You can also use these earlier parts of your solos as a chance to form a repeating "motif" or a central idea you can build around. We want our solos to remind us of the main *melodies* of jazz songs, which *do not have to be complicated.* Take "C Jam Blues," a classic 12-bar blues that literally consists of two notes. Check out how, after a blistering 2.5-minute solo, this Oscar Peterson live version[6] breaks into that uber-simple head. Or, check out the simple motif-building at the

---

[4] https://www.youtube.com/watch?v=vVwEeiyPfFg&t=547s&ab_channel=8-bitMusicTheory

[5] https://www.youtube.com/watch?v=ItIqoBR0cP8&t=147s&ab_channel=8-bitMusicTheory

[6] https://www.youtube.com/watch?v=NTJhHn-TuDY&t=152s&ab_channel=dgbailey777

beginning of the piano solo in "The Sidewinder[7]." It gets a bit more complex as the solo builds, but it's all based on repeating motifs. And don't forget, you can also "quote" famous licks, melodies, or songs - pop culture references in music form (both inside *and* outside jazz).

Eventually, soloing will reach a heightened point of difficulty - for instance, songs at high tempos with chord changes that are anything *but* diatonic. A classic example is "Giant Steps."[8] - its scales frequently move an "augmented 2nd" away from each other (also considered a "minor 3rd" enharmonically - "enharmonic" being music speaks for "same pitch, different name"). Hence the name of the song. This song is considered a sort of "rite of passage" for jazz soloists due to its difficulty. But if you work your way up from the blues, modal, and more diatonically-oriented songs, it will become more approachable based on your built-up knowledge and experience.

Plus, even Giant Steps uses other mini-patterns of chord changes that we will see pop up regularly and become more familiar with. One common pattern we see at the end of phrases in lots of jazz (and even pop music) is the ii-V-I.

---

[7] https://www.youtube.com/watch?v=qJi03NqXfk8&t=332s&ab_channel=JazzTuna
[8] https://www.youtube.com/watch?v=30FTr6G53VU&ab_channel=Jazzman2696

Chapter 8.5

Improvisation 2.5: The "ii-V-I"

A *very* common pattern to see at the end of a section of music is the ii-V-I - pronounced "Two, Five, One." As it sounds, this ending consists of a "two-chord," a "five-chord," and a "one-chord." If we were in C major, this would amount to a Dm7, a G7, and a Cmaj7, or these chords/scales:

D e **F** g **A** b **C**

G a **B** c **D** e **F**

C d **E** f **G** a **B**

It's definitely in your best interest to get acquainted with this mini-progression in as many keys as possible since it's *so* common. Try to find lines that connect these scales musically in whatever key you're playing. The minor key version is slightly different since the minor scale changes some notes. In a major key, these are the diatonic chords (we'll use C major as our jumping-off scale):

I - CEG

ii - DFA

iii - EGB

IV - FAC

V - GBD

vi - ACE

vii° - BDF

If we add a (diatonic) 7th to each chord, as is typical in jazz, we get these chords:

Cmaj7 - CEGB

Dmin7 - DFAC

Emin7 - EGBD

Fmaj7 - FACE

G7 - GBDF

Amin7 - ACEG

Bmin7b5 - BDFA (also known as B-half-diminished)

But our C *minor* scale is different - it flattens the third, sixth, and seventh scale degrees - although the **"five"** chord often still ends up as a major to **"grandfather in"** the leading tone (or major seventh of the original scale). So, diatonically, our C *minor* chords end up looking like this:

Cmin7	C Eb G Bb
Dmin7b5	D F Ab C
Ebmaj7	Eb G Bb D
Fmin7	F Ab C Eb
*G7	G B D F
Abmaj7	Ab C Eb G
Bb7	Bb D F Ab

The five-chord *should* be a Gmin7, spelled out as G Bb D F. But again - we just *love* a 5-chord to contain its own major third in it, as that makes us want to return to the root since it's a half-step away. Another semi-contemporary example of this can be found in <u>many</u>[9], <u>many</u>[10] <u>Muse</u>[11] songs. So many, in fact, that I just call this the "Muse chord" - essentially, it's just a major V chord in any minor song.

Now that we've done a crash course in diatonic chords for minor keys, here's our minor ii-V-i:

Dm7b5	D F Ab C
G7	G B D F
Cm7	C Eb G Bb

---

[9] https://www.youtube.com/watch?v=lq_W19qo-X8&ab_channel=KieransMuse
[10] https://www.youtube.com/watch?v=3dm_5qWWDV8&ab_channel=Muse
[11] https://www.youtube.com/watch?v=MCr36u4i_7E&list=OLAK5uy_lGTmzBZksrZO015dx4U8mDTjkAQJdtuTE&index=2&ab_channel=Muse-Topic

Let's transpose that to G minor:

Am7b5   A C Eb G

D7   D F A C

Gmin7   G Bb D F

Oh, look at that! That's the chord progression from the end of "Fly Me to the Moon" we covered earlier! In a way, that D7 wasn't even un-diatonic (technically, it was - but it gets that lack-of-weirdness "pass" that a Major-5-chord gets in minor keys).

Let's try another tactic quickly here. Let's analyze the chord changes to "White Christmas" in our key of C. Look at how daunting these changes look! They're terrifying!

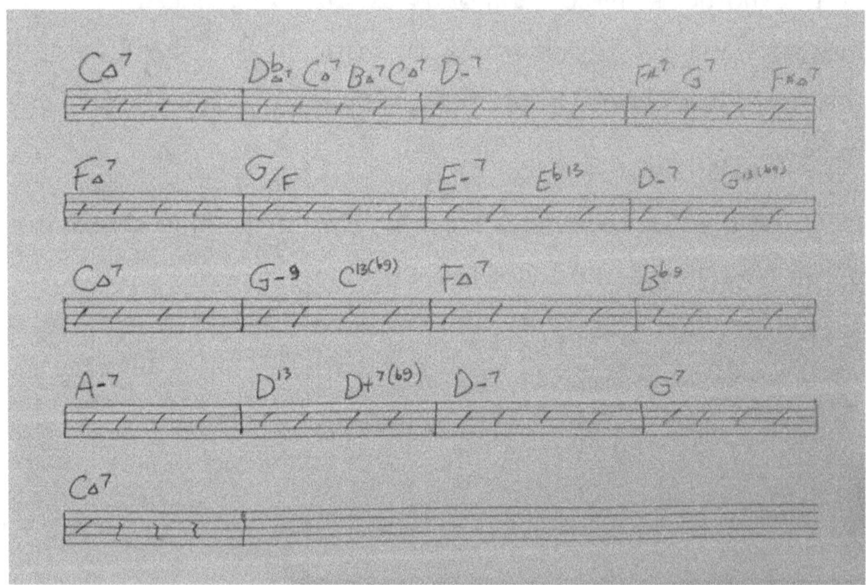

I actually had a student recently take a solo over this for a winter concert. Even the pre-written option was intimidating to him, and trying to digest a crash course in improvisation in a matter of weeks was certainly a bridge too far. But how complicated are these changes, *really?*

We start with a C-major-7 (just a reminder, the triangle-7 means "major-7"). This makes sense, as it's a diatonic "one" chord. The second measure *looks* scary, but in reality, the chords just vacillate chromatically around the C-major-7 - first, by hitting the note above C (Db), then returning to C, then dipping below C (to B), then returning once again to C. Entire major-7 chords are built on top of these chromatic vacillations. This matches the melody of the song, at the point of the lyrics "Dreaming of a" - so it's easy to remember where/when this happens. And, if you're improvising, you basically are safe to land on any chord tone of your C-major-7 at the end of the first measure and then chromatically surround that chord tone in the second measure. OR - you can simply ignore this chromatic wibble-wobble and do your own thing on C-major-7! If you own your choices with swagger, you can somewhat get away with what you want!

Then, if we look at the third and fourth measures - really, it's just another ii-V. The V is just adorned with a chromatic approach - there's an F#7 on beat one, but it's really just an ornament on the real meat of the measure - the G7 (or V-chord). The timing of *this* chromatic approach is easy to anticipate and remember because it's reflected in the melody of the lyrics "*Christ*-mas." Then, we have a Fmaj7 chord in the 5th measure - the F#maj7 on beat 4 of the previous measure is just an ornament and/or approach to the Fmaj7.

We don't need to keep spelling out *all* the other simplifications that are going on in the soloist's mind in the text - we'll write them out in these updated chord changes attached instead. I'll include the bigger chord changes that you'll want to hit, as well as what calculations are happening mentally to simplify the changes:

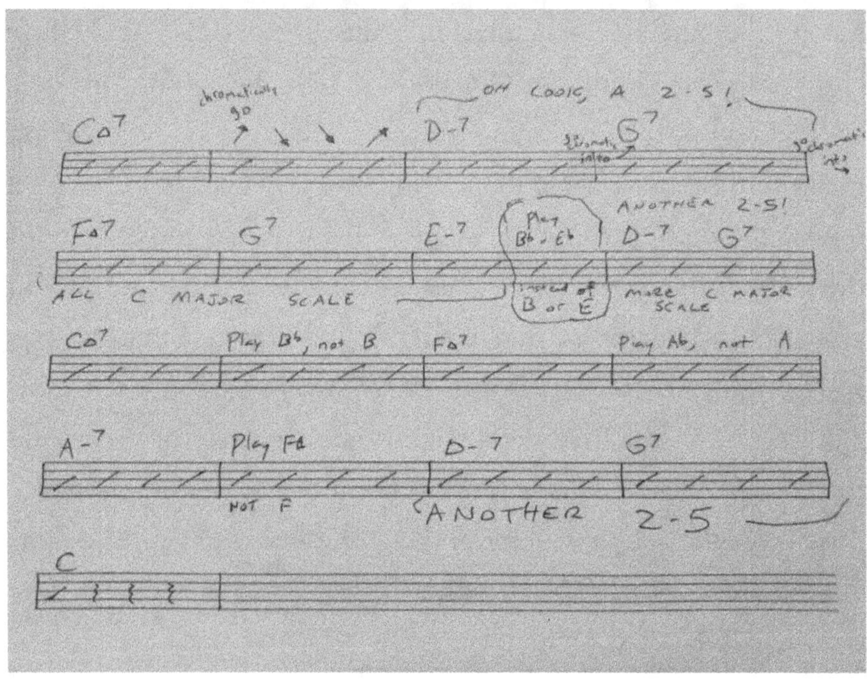

Just about all of the non-diatonic chord changes are semi-optional - especially the chromatic approaches to the next chord. You can blow through them with the good old C-major scale with bluster and good melodic ideas! Plus, over time, you'll start stacking "licks" that you can bust out in a variety of situations - like ii-V-Is. And, even with *all* of the changes, most of these are just diatonic chords, and the C major scale would work *anyway*.

Here's an example of the Author soloing over "White Christmas" using these chord changes (in the trumpet key of C - concert Bb - as usual, these chords are the ones *we're* reading from for *our* key). Our Author is very out of shape in trumpet improvisation, but these simplifying calculations make soloing over this song *way* easier than it looks.

Audio Example: 15. White Christmas Solo

One last tool that should be in every trumpeter's belt, *especially* if they want to improvise, is the book Technical Studies for the Cornet by H.L. Clarke. Every trumpet player should work through these exercises, but *especially* improvisers and anyone interested in playing jazz. I touched on this in earlier trumpet and cornet books, but let's look at some of the patterns they want you to do in the first three studies alone (I'll include our key of C major from each study):

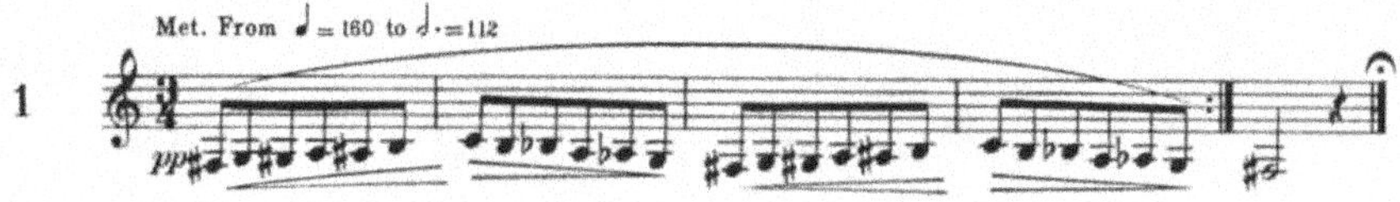

The first study gets you very well-equipped to use the chromatic scale - it teaches you all of the "universal" fingerings of the trumpet, as I call them. As mentioned earlier, the chromatic scale will be useful both because chromatic approaches happen so often in jazz music and because it can get you out of a jam when soloing.

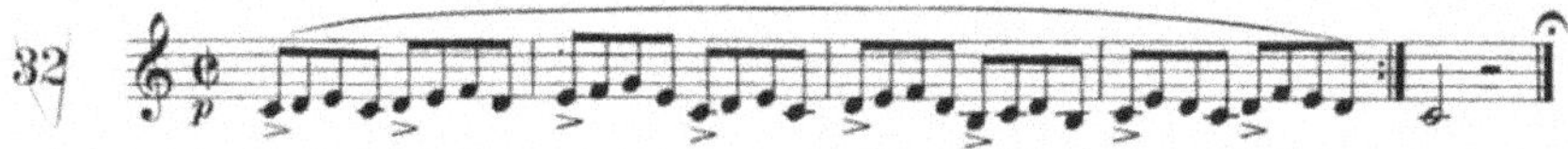

This second study gets you used to a very common pattern for use in improvised solos as well as written melodies. I closed out my "White Christmas" solo with this pattern as 16th notes (go figure) and only half-realized what I was doing.

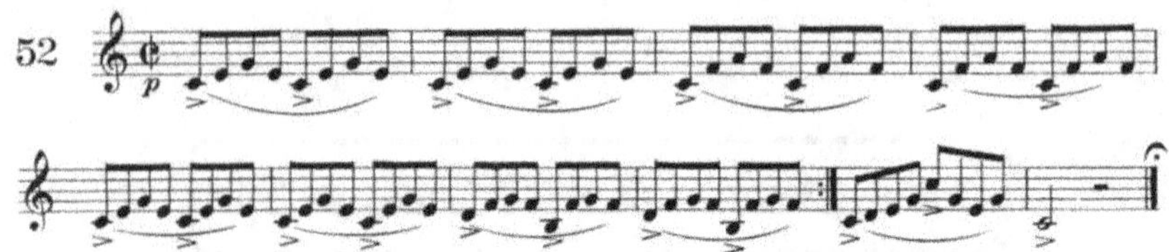

Check out the third study. It's clearly having you play an arpeggio, but look at what notes it moves to throughout the drill. CEG in the first two measures - got it, that's a C-major arpeggio, makes total sense. But then CFA in the third and fourth measures - if we invert that, we get FAC - aka, an F major chord. That's our IV-chord, but inverted so that it's in a more similar position to the I-chord. Then, it returns to CEG. After that, we get DFGFBFGF - oh, look at that, if we put those notes in order, we get GBDF. It takes our familiar V7 chord but again inverts it to be in a similar range as our I chord. All of this is *extremely* useful for improvisation, as we often have to connect these very chords to each other without jumping awkwardly (i.e., in a connecting melody).

All these studies are run through all 12 keys, and some keys even get multiple exercises to cover different octaves. Then they culminate in an "etude" that weaves throughout multiple keys (in my experience, "etude" really means "combination of song and exercise," as far as musical academia is concerned).

Hopefully, that wasn't too much music theory - but even if you have no interest in improvisation, there's still some skimmable info you might find helpful. Still, no worries if you skipped it altogether. At the end of the day, music theory isn't as complicated as it sounds - it's all simple math and basically just the *labeling* of what we all hear, regardless of our education levels. I find it interesting, but I'm a nerd (and you don't have to be to play jazz!). If you have any further questions about how music theory works, a killer resource for that is musictheory.net. It's a fairly dry website but it has all the lessons and exercises you need to fully understand this stuff (including relative majors and minors - something we barely covered here). Even if you go out and get yourself a fancy music degree, chances are your school will just be sending you here all the time, anyway.

Some more random thoughts:

If you want to play in a big band, you'll need to find 17 co-conspirators, which may be a tough sell. Again, big bands are typically institutions in and of themselves and operated through existing structures. But there may be big local bands you can join through community centers, recreational hubs, and community colleges - you don't need to be Dizzy Gillespie to find a big band to play with! Just like you don't need to be Cristiano Ronaldo to find an adult recreational soccer league.

Wherever you find them, these big band jazz groups will provide you with sheet music and repertoire to play. But if you want to play small group jazz, you'll need to find the songs to play yourself. Enter "The Real Book" to the rescue!

Chapter 9

"The Real Book" - 400 Songs to Get You Started

Remember those lead sheets we mentioned before? "The Real Book" is the gold standard anthology every jazz musician needs to own.

It's called that as a play on "Fake Book" - as in the idea that lead sheets are a way to "fake" your way through songs. Each lead sheet contains just the melody and chord changes of the song, and small groups typically follow the format mentioned above - everyone plays the "head" (main melody) once, they optionally repeat it with either the saxophone or trumpet playing harmonies, everyone takes an improvised solo the length of one or more "choruses" (times through the melody), and then the melody is played again to end the song.

This "Real Book" was actually a completely black market item until relatively recently. Nearly all the songs are "standards" (old-timey jazz and pop classics), but it still wasn't at all legal due to copyright issues. Eventually, Hal Leonard bought most of this material and dropped the songs for which it didn't secure licenses, and The Real Book as it exists now is 100% legal and available at any major (music) retailer. The 5th Edition is even available online for free http://www.play-along.ch/notationz/Volume1Bb.pdf[12] (this link goes to the Bb version for trumpeters).

---

[12] http://www.play-along.ch/notationz/Volume1Bb.pdf

We've already covered plenty of songs that make great starter tracks to play over, but we can re-list them here for ease of use. These songs are a great jumping-off point and are so well-known that it's pretty easy to find original recordings to play with online, *as well as* instrumental backing tracks with lead instruments taken out. Just a reminder that every one of them is available in the free, online 5th Edition of The Real Book, which can be found at the link above:

Beginner songs to both *play* and *improvise over*:

"C Jam Blues"

"So What?"

"Straight No Chaser"

"Blue Monk"

"All Blues"

"Freddie the Freeloader"

"Four"

"Song for My Father"

"Afro Blue"

"Maiden Voyage"

Intermediate songs to both *play* and *improvise over*:

"Confirmation" (this one might be a bit more on the advanced side, actually - especially at higher tempos)

"Au Privave"

"Blue Bossa"

"All of Me"

"Jordu"

"Take Five"

"Take the A-Train"

"Well, You Needn't"

"Ornithology"

"Oleo"

"Joy Spring"

"A Night in Tunisia"

Beginner songs to *play*, but intermediate to *improvise over*.

"Fly Me to the Moon"

"Autumn Leaves"

"It Don't Mean a Thing (If It Ain't Got That Swing)"

"All the Things You Are"

"Don't Get Around Much Anymore"

"Solar"

"Girl from Ipanema"

Intermediate songs to *play*, but easy to *improvise over*.

"The Sidewinder" (simply due to the range of the "head" - it's still pretty easy to play if you can hit high notes).

Whether these songs are intermediate or beginner-level is clearly subjective, and my classifications may not line up with yours. If you find something harder than I've listed here, no worries; it's probably just a difference of opinion! You're not "behind" or anything. And if you find it easier than I've labeled it, congrats! You're objectively ahead of the curve! Take a glass-half-full approach.

Remember that if you decide to play over backing tracks on these songs, they need to be in the same key that they're listed in for it to sound good. Since these songs are "standards," most of which have been played and recorded by *many* artists, there will thus be many versions of these songs floating around - and they could be in different keys than the ones listed.

But you're now ready to go! You've got all the tools to play in a big band or a small group and to improvise in both settings over a variety of chord changes. Go forth and play the original American genre, jazz! It's easier than it sounds and just as rewarding!

Unlock Your Musical Potential:
Get 30% Off the Next Step in Your
Instrumental Journey

As a token of appreciation for your dedication, we're excited to offer you an **exclusive 30% discount** on your next product when you sign up below with your email address.

Visit the link below:

https://bit.ly/40NikR2

OR

Use the QR Code:

Unlocking your musical potential is easier with ongoing guidance and support. Join our community of passionate musicians to elevate your skills and stay updated with the latest tips and tricks. By signing up, you'll also receive our periodic newsletter with additional insights and resources to enhance your musical journey.

Your privacy is important to us. We won't spam you, and you can unsubscribe anytime.

Don't miss out on this opportunity to continue your musical journey with this special discount. Sign up now, and let's embark on this musical adventure together! 🎼